The Big Book Of New Testament Bible Trivia

Cheryl Pryor

Arlington & Amelia Publishing

Copyright © 2018 Cheryl Pryor

Arlington & Amelia Publishing

All rights reserved. No portion of this book may be reproduced or transmitted in any form or by any means, electronic or mechanical, including photocopy, recording, or any information storage and retrieval system without permission of the author.

ISBN-10: 1-886541-34-5
ISBN-13: 978-1-886541-34-4

TABLE OF CONTENTS

Gospels — 1

1. Matthew — 2
   Answers on page 9
2. Mark — 14
   Answers on page 17
3. Luke — 19
   Answers on page 25
4. John — 29
   Answers on page 32

Acts / Church History — 34

5. Acts — 35
   Answers on page 39

Paul's Letters — 41

6. Romans — 42
   Answers on page 44
7. First Corinthians — 45
   Answers on page 47
8. Second Corinthians — 48
   Answers on page 49
9. Galatians — 50

Answers on page 51

10	Ephesians	52

Answers on page 53

11	Philippians	54

Answers on page 55

12	Colossians	56

Answers on page 57

13	First Thessalonians	58

Answers on page 59

14	Second Thessalonians	60

Answers on page 61

15	First Timothy	62

Answers on page 63

16	Second Timothy	64

Answers on page 65

17	Titus	66

Answers on page 67

18	Philemon	68

Answers on page 69

Non-Pauline Letters — 70

19	Hebrews	71

Answers on page 73

20	James	74

Answers on page 77

21	First Peter	79

Answers on page 80

22	Second Peter	81

Answers on page 82

23	First John	83

Answers on page 85

24	Second John	86

Answers on page 87

25	Third John	88

Answers on page 89

26	Jude	90

Answers on page 91

Apocalypse 92

27	Revelations	93

Answers on page 94

For Perry

Who led me to Christ

> Let your light shine before men in such a way that they may see your good works, and glorify your Father who is in Heaven.
>
> - Matthew 5: 18

- Scriptures in this book are from the New American Standard Bible

OTHER BOOKS BY CHERYL PRYOR

The Big Book of Old Testament Bible Trivia

The Big Book of Presidential Trivia

The Big Book of First Ladies Trivia

Presidents, First Ladies, & First Family Trivia

Presidents Trivia Challenge

First Family Trivia

American Revolution & The Birth of A Nation Trivia

Living The Word of God

Chosen

Children Of The Presidents

Pregnancy Journal

Precious Moments

Treasured Moments of My Child

My Mother's Life Story

My Father's Life Story

How Much Do You *Really* Know About The Love Of Your Life?

Couples Game Night Challenge

RV Travel & Expense Journal

Wedding Survival Guide

Write Now

Legacy

Children's Books

My Child's Keepsake Journal

Trivia For Kids: The Presidents

Trivia For Kids: First Ladies

From the series: The Sullivan Family Series

Savannah In The Big Move

Savannah On Stage

Savannah On Horseback

Savannah in Look What Followed Me Home

Savannah & The Grumpy Neighbor

Savannah & The Mad Scientist

From the series: Savannah's World Travels Series

Savannah's Disney World Celebration

Savannah Goes To Paris

Gospels

MATTHEW

Answers on page 9

1. The genealogy of Jesus (the Messiah, the son of David, the son of Abraham) is traced back to Mary or Joseph?

2. Betrothed to Mary, what was Joseph's initial plan concerning Mary when he discovered she was with child?

3. What changed Joseph's mind concerning his original plan?

4. Where was Jesus born?

5. Who was king at the time of Jesus birth?

6. Who were the magi searching for?

7. How did the magi find Jesus?

8. What gifts did the magi bring?

9. What did God warn the magi of in a dream?

10. After the magi left an angel appeared to Joseph in a dream. What was the angel's message?

11. How long did Joseph, Mary, and Jesus remain in Egypt?

12. What was Herod's reaction to bring tricked by the magi, by them not returning and revealing the whereabouts of the Christ child?

13. Twice more after the death of Herod, Joseph received messages in a dream. Leaving Egypt, where did he take his family fulfilling the word of the prophets?

14. What message was John the Baptist preaching?

15. What food did John the Baptist sustain himself with out in the wilderness?

16. Where was John the Baptist baptizing the people as they confessed their sins?

17. What did John the Baptist call the Pharisees and the Sadducees?

18. When John the Baptist baptized Jesus, when Jesus came up from the water the heavens were opened and John saw the Spirit of God descending as a dove and lighting on Jesus. God's voice from out of the heavens said what at this time?

19. Who tempted Jesus during his time in the wilderness?

20. How many days and nights did Jesus fast while in the wilderness?

21. What was Jesus' response to the devil when he told Jesus to throw

Himself down from the pinnacle of the temple with the devil quoting that God would command His angels concerning Him?

22. When Jesus began His ministry, where did He settle?

23. Who were the first disciples who were brothers that were fishing at the Sea of Galilee?

24. From the Sermon on the Mount, what did Jesus teach about the pure in heart?

25. How did Jesus encourage those who were persecuted because of Him?

26. What was Jesus' teachings about one who was angry with his brother?

27. What does Jesus say you should do concerning your enemies?

28. What are we instructed to do when we give to the poor?

29. *Fill in the blanks.* The Lord's Prayer. 'Our Father who is in Heaven, Hallowed be Your name. Your kingdom come, Your _____ be done, On earth as it is in heaven. Give us this day our daily bread, And forgive us our debts, as we also have forgiven our debtors. And do not lead us into temptation, but deliver us from _____. For Yours is the kingdom and the power and the glory forever. Amen.

30. What does the Bible teach in regards to if we forgive others for their transgressions?

31. *Fill in the blank.* Do not worry about tomorrow; for tomorrow will care

for itself. Each day has enough _____ of its own.

32. *Fill in the blank.* "Why do you look at the speck that is in your brother's eye, but do not notice the _____ that is in your own eye?"

33. What is the Law and the Prophets found in Matthew 7: 12? Some refer to this as the Golden Rule.

34. Who does Jesus say will enter the kingdom of heaven?

35. A man who does what, may be compared to a wise man who built his house on the rock?

36. Why did Jesus marvel at the centurion who asked Jesus to heal his servant? Jesus said to his followers, "Truly, I say to you, I have not found such great faith with anyone in Israel."

37. How did Jesus fulfill Isaiah's prophecy, "He Himself took our infirmities and carried away our diseases"?

38. There were two men who were demon possessed in the country of Gadarenes, the demons entreated Jesus to do what with them?

39. What was Matthew's livelihood?

40. What was Jesus' response when He heard the Pharisees asking His disciples why He ate with tax collectors and sinners?

41. The woman suffering for twelve years with a hemorrhage told herself if she could just touch the fringe of His cloak she would be healed. What did Jesus say made her well?

42. As Jesus rose the dead, healed the blind, and sick; what did the Pharisees say as to why He was able to cast out demons?

43. Who did Jesus give authority over unclean spirits to, so they were able to cast them out and to heal every kind of disease and sickness?

44. What are the names of the 12 apostles?

45. *Fill in the blank.* The words Jesus spoke to His disciples as He sent them out to preach and heal to the lost sheep of the house of Israel: "I send you out as _____ in the midst of wolves; so be shrewd as _____ and innocent as _____."

46. Who was the prophesy below referring to as the messenger? "Behold, I send My messenger ahead of You, who will prepare Your way before You."

47. What is the unpardonable sin?

48. *Fill in the blank.* The mouth speaks out of that which fills the _____.

49. In what way will people be accountable for every careless word they speak?

50. *Fill in the blanks.* For whoever does the will of My Father who is in heaven, he is My _____ and _____ and _____.

51. In the parable of the sower, what did Jesus say would happen to the seed sown in good soil?

52. Why did Herod have John the Baptist arrested?

53. Why did Herod have John the Baptist beheaded?

54. Jesus asked His disciples, "Who do the people say that the Son of Man is?" He then asked them, "Who do you say that I am?" How did Simon Peter answer?

55. *Fill in the blank.* Jesus said, "Unless you are converted and become like _____, you will not enter the kingdom of heaven."

56. Who did the Son of Man say He had come to save?

57. *Fill in the blank.* It is easier for a camel to go through the eye of a needle, than for a _____ man to enter the kingdom of God.

58. Jesus told His disciples they were going to Jerusalem where He would be crucified. What did He say would happen to Him on the third day?

59. *Fill in the blank.* Many are called, but few are _____.

60. What is the great and foremost commandment?

61. What is the second great commandment – the two commandments which depend the whole Law and the Prophets?

62. *Fill in the blank.* You will be hearing of wars and _____ of wars.

63. Who knows when Jesus will return?

64. Which of the disciples betrayed Jesus?

65. What did the disciple who betrayed Jesus receive as payment for his betrayal?

66. At the Last Passover, how did Jesus reveal which disciple would betray Him?

67. What was Judas' fate after betraying Jesus?

68. Where was Jesus crucified?

69. In whose tomb was Jesus buried?

70. When Mary Magdalene and the other Mary came to the grave of Jesus, what did the angel from heaven tell the women?

71. What was the Great Commission Jesus gave to His disciples after He had risen from the dead?

Answers – Chapter 1 – Matthew

1. Joseph, the husband of Mary, by whom Jesus was born. - Matthew 1: 1 – 16

2. He planned to send her away, not wanting to disgrace her. - Matthew 1: 18 – 19

3. An angel of the Lord appeared to him in a dream telling him the child she carried was conceived by the Holy Spirit. - Matthew 1: 20

4. Bethlehem - Matthew 2: 1

5. Herod - Matthew 2: 1

6. He who was born King of the Jews. - Matthew 2: 2

7. They followed the star in the east. - Matthew 2: 7 – 10

8. Gold, frankincense, and myrrh - Matthew 2: 11

9. Not to return to Herod - Matthew 2: 12

10. To take the child and his mother and flee to Egypt and remain there until the angel told him to leave, as Herod was searching for the child to kill him. - Matthew 2: 13

11. Until the death of Herod - Matthew 2: 14

12. He became enraged and ordered all male children in Bethlehem and it's vicinity, that were two years old and under to be killed. - Matthew 2: 16 – 18

13. Nazarene, "He shall be called a Nazarene." - Matthew 2: 19 – 23

14. To repent, for the kingdom of heaven is at hand. - Matthew 3: 1 – 2

15. Locusts and wild honey - Matthew 3: 4

16. Jordan River - Matthew 3: 5 – 6

17. Brood of vipers - Matthew 3: 7

18. "This is My beloved Son, in whom I am well-pleased." - Matthew 3: 13 – 17

19. The devil - Matthew 4: 1

20. 40 days and 40 nights - Matthew 4: 2

21. "You shall not put the Lord Your God to the test." - Matthew 4: 5 – 7

22. Capernaum (by the sea in the region of Zebulon and Naphtali - Matthew 4: 12 – 13

23. Simon called Peter and his brother Andrew - Matthew 4: 18 – 19

24. They shall see God - Matthew 5: 8

25. Their reward in heaven is great. - Matthew 5: 11 – 12

26. They were guilty and should be reconciled to his brother. - Matthew 5: 21 – 24

27. Leave your enemies and pray for those who persecute you. - Matthew 5: 44

28. Do not let your left hand know what your right hand is doing, so your giving will be in secret and your Father will reward you. - Matthew 6: 2 – 4

29. Will, evil - Matthew 6: 9 – 13

30. Then our heavenly Father will forgive us. - Matthew 6: 14 – 15

31. Trouble - Matthew 6: 34

32. Log - Matthew 7: 3

33. Treat people the same way you want them to treat you. - Matthew 7: 12

34. "He who does the will of My Father who is in heaven." - Matthew 7: 21

35. Those who hears the words of Jesus and acts on these words. - Matthew 7: 24

36. He told Jesus he was unworthy for Him to come under his roof, but to just say the word and he knew his servant would be healed. - Matthew 8: 5 – 13

37. Healing those sick and demon-possessed and those who were blind and lame. - Matthew 8: 14 – 17

38. Cast them into the swine - Matthew 8: 28 – 32

39. Tax collector - Matthew 9: 9

40. He didn't come to call the righteous, but sinners. - Matthew 9: 10 – 13

41. Her faith - Matthew 9: 20 – 22

42. The Pharisees said, "He casts out the demons by the ruler of the demons." - Matthew 9: 18 – 35

43. His disciples - Matthew 10: 1

44. Simon called Peter, Andrew, James, John, Philip, Bartholomew, Thomas, Matthew, James, Thaddeus, Simon, and Judas - Matthew 10: 2 – 4

45. Sheep, serpents, doves - Matthew 10: 5 – 16

46. John the Baptist - Matthew 11: 7 – 10

47. Blasphemy against the Spirit - Matthew 12: 31 – 32

48. Heart - Matthew 12: 34

49. They shall give an accounting for it in the day of judgment. For by your words you will be justified, and by your words you will be condemned. - Matthew 12: 36 – 37

50. Brother, sister, mother - Matthew 12: 50

51. He referred it to the man who hears the word and understands it and bears fruit. - Matthew 13: 18 – 23

52. John told him it was unlawful for him to have Herodias, the wife of his brother. - Matthew 14: 3 – 4

53. On his birthday, the daughter of Herodias danced for him and pleased him. He offered her anything she wanted. Prompted by Herodias, her mother, she asked for the head of John the Baptist on a platter. - Matthew 14: 6 – 10

54. "You are the Christ, the Son of the living God." - Matthew 16: 13 – 16

55. Children - Matthew 18: 1 – 3

56. The lost - Matthew 18: 11

57. Rich - Matthew 19: 24

58. He would be raised up - Matthew 20: 18 – 19

59. Chosen - Matthew 22: 14

60. You shall love the Lord your God with all your heart, and with all your soul, and with all your mind. - Matthew 22: 36 – 38

61. You shall love your neighbor as yourself - Matthew 22: 39 – 40

62. Rumors - Matthew 24: 6

63. "Of that day and hour no one knows, not even the angels of heaven, nor the Son, but the Father alone." - Matthew 24: 32 – 39

64. Judas Iscariot - Matthew 26: 14 – 15

65. 30 pieces of silver - Matthew 26: 14 – 15

66. He told the disciples, "He who dipped his hand with Me in the bowl is the one who will betray Me." - Matthew 26: 20 – 23

67. He was remorseful and returned the 30 pieces of silver and hung himself. - Matthew 27: 3 – 5

68. Golgotha (Jerusalem) - Matthew 27: 33

69. Joseph from Arimathea - Matthew 27: 57 – 60

70. He has risen from the dead. - Matthew 28: 1 – 7

71. "Make disciples of all the nations, baptizing them in the name of the Father and the Son and the Holy Spirit, teaching them to observe all that I commanded you." - Matthew 28: 16 – 20

2

MARK

Answers on page 17

1. John the Baptist preached in the wilderness a baptism of repentance of what?

2. What type of clothing did John the Baptist wear?

3. During the 40 days Jesus spent fasting in the wilderness and being tempted by Satan, who ministered to Him?

4. Which disciples of Jesus were brothers?

5. Were the demons aware of who Jesus was?

6. What name is Levi the son of Alphaeus most commonly known as?

7. What other name was given to the brothers James and John?

8. When Jesus asked the man with an unclean spirit in Gerasenes what his name was, what was the man's response?

9. What did the synagogue official named Jarius request of Jesus?

10. Before Jairus and Jesus arrived at the home of Jairus, they received word that his daughter had died. What was Jesus' response?

11. How did the people respond when Jesus went to his hometown and began to teach in the synagogue?

12. Who did King Herod think Jesus was?

13. When the disciples were out to sea straining against the winds and the oars, why did they think Jesus was a ghost when they saw Him?

14. *Fill in the blank.* All things are possible to him who _____.

15. *Fill in the blank.* He who is not _____ us is for us.

16. Who did Jesus drive out from the temple?

17. When Christ returns, the sun will be darkened and the moon will not give its light, what will be falling from heaven?

18. At the last Passover, at the Lord's Supper, what did Christ tell the disciples the bread and the wine were?

19. Which of the disciples did Jesus tell that he would deny Him three times that night before a rooster crowed twice?

20. What did Jesus pray in Gethsemane?

21. How did Judas betray Jesus?

22. How did the Roman cohort mock Jesus?

23. Who was pressed into service to bear Jesus' cross?

24. At what place was Jesus crucified?

Answers – Chapter 2 – Mark

1. Repentance for the forgiveness of sins – Mark 1: 4

2. Clothing made of camel's hair and a leather belt – Mark 1: 6

3. Angels – Mark 1: 13

4. Simon (Peter) and Andrew were brothers and James and John were also brothers. – Mark 1: 16 – 20

5. Yes – Mark 1: 34

6. Matthew – Mark 2: 14

7. Boanerges, which means 'Sons of Thunder' – Mark 3: 17

8. "My name is Legion; for we are many." – Mark 5: 1 – 16

9. For Jesus to lay His hands on his daughter who was near death so she would get well and live – Mark 5: 22

10. He told Jairus to believe, entered the house and told those in mourning the girl was only asleep. He entered her room, took her by the hand, and told her to get up. She did. – Mark 5: 35 – 43

11. The people were astonished and took offense. – Mark 6: 1 – 4

12. John the Baptist risen – Mark 6: 14 – 16

13. He was walking on the water. – Mark 6: 45 – 52

14. Believes – Mark 9: 23

15. Against – Mark 9: 40

16. Those who were buying and selling in the temple. – Mark 11: 15

17. The stars – Mark 13: 24 – 25

18. The bread He told his disciples was His body and the wine His blood.

– Mark 14: 22 – 24

19. Peter – Mark 14: 27 – 31

20. That if it were possible the hour might pass Him by and asked His Father to remove this cup from Him; yet not what He willed, but what God willed. – Mark 14: 32 – 36

21. With a kiss – Mark 14: 43 – 45

22. They dressed Him in purple with a crown of thorns calling Him 'King of the Jews,' bowing before Him and bowing and spitting on Him. – Mark 15: 16 – 19

23. Simon of Cyrene – Mark 15: 21

24. Golgotha – Mark 15: 22 – 25

3

LUKE

Answers on page 25

1. What were the names of the parents of John the Baptist?

2. How was the birth of John the Baptist foretold to his father?

3. What did the angel reveal to Zacharius about his son?

4. What was the angel's name who came before Zacharias?

5. What happened to Zacharias because he didn't believe the angel's words?

6. What was the name of the angel who appeared to Mary?

7. What did the angel tell Mary?

8. Mary found the angels statement perplexing, what was Mary's question to the angel?

9. How did the angel respond to how she would conceive the Son of God?

10. When Mary visited Elizabeth and she heard Mary's greeting, what occurred?

11. Who sent out a decree for a census to be taken of all the inhabited earth in the days that Mary was heavy with child?

12. After the birth of Jesus, who did an angel of the Lord and a multitude of the heavenly host appear before to bring the news that the Savior, Christ the Lord was born?

13. What action did the shepherds take after the angels departed?

14. A man in Jerusalem, righteous and devout and filled with the Holy Spirit, took Jesus in his arms in the temple and proclaimed to God that he had seen His salvation. What was this man's name?

15. Where did Mary and Joseph go every year for the Feast of the Passover?

16. What age was Jesus when after celebrating the Feast of the Passover on the return trip home Mary and Joseph discovered Jesus was missing?

17. When Jesus was discovered missing Mary and Joseph returned to Jerusalem and found Jesus. Where was He and what was He doing?

18. *Fill in the blanks.* John told the crowds coming to hear him preach that he baptized with _____, and told them One was coming that would baptize them with the _____ _____ and _____.

19. At what age was Jesus when He began His ministry?

20. Which of the disciples was called 'the Zealot'?

21. *Fill in the blank.* From the Beatitudes: Blessed are you who are _____, for yours is the kingdom of God.

22. *Fill in the blanks.* Love your enemies, and do good, and lend, expecting _____ in return; and your reward will be _____.

23. *Fill in the blank.* His mouth speaks that which fills his _____.

24. Who was Jesus referring to when He said, "I say to you, not even in Israel have I found such great faith"?

25. Who was Jesus referring to when He said, "Among those born of women there is no one greater; yet He who is least in the kingdom of God is greater than he"?

26. When Jesus accepted the invitation to dine at the home of the Pharisee there was a woman there who was a great sinner who wept at His feet and wiped them with her hair, kissing them and anointing them with perfume. When the Pharisee witnessed this he said, "If Jesus were a prophet He would know the sort of woman she was." How did Jesus respond?

27. Mary, who was called Magdalene, had been filled with how many demons?

28. How many were fed from 5 loaves and 2 fish?

29. During the Transfiguration, what two men did Peter, John, and James witness speaking to Jesus?

30. Jesus appointed 70 and sent them out to heal the sick and proclaim, "The kingdom of God has come near to you." When the 70 returned joyous that even the demons were subject to them in Jesus name, Jesus told them not to rejoice in the fact that the spirits were subject to them, but to rejoice in what?

31. When a man asked Jesus what he must do to inherit eternal life he was told, "You shall love your God with all your heart, all your soul, with all your strength, and with all your mind; and your neighbor as yourself." When the man asked who his neighbor was, what parable did Jesus tell him as an example?

32. When one of the disciples asked Jesus to teach them to pray as John the Baptist had taught his disciples, what did Jesus tell them to pray?

33. *Fill in the blank.* Ask, and it will be given to you; _____, and you will find; Knock, and it will be opened to you.

34. *Fill in the blank.* Blessed are those who hear the word of God and _____ it.

35. *Fill in the blank.* Watch out that the light in you is not darkness. If therefore your whole body is full of light, with no _____ part in it, it will be wholly illumined, as when the lamp illumines you with its rays.

36. *Fill in the blank.* There is nothing covered up that will not be _____, and hidden that will not be known. Whatever you have said in the dark will be heard in the light, and what you have whispered in the inner rooms will be proclaimed upon the housetops and revealed.

37. What two things did Jesus use to compare what the kingdom of God was like?

38. *Fill in the blank.* There is joy in the presence of the angels of God over one sinner who _____.

39. Why was the father joyous over his son who had left home and squandered his inheritance, when he returned home?

40. Who was Jesus speaking to when He said, "You are those who justify yourselves in the sight of men, but God knows your hearts; for that which is highly esteemed among men is detestable in the sight of God"?

41. *Fill in the blank.* If your brother sins, rebuke him; and if he repents, _____ him.

42. *Fill in the blanks.* Everyone who exalts himself will be _____, but he who _____ himself will be exalted.

43. *Fill in the blank.* Heaven and earth will pass away, but My _____ will not pass away.

44. Why did Jesus say to partake of the Lord's Supper?

45. *Fill in the blank.* In the garden of Gethsemane, Jesus prayed fervently; and his sweat became like drops of _____.

46. After Jesus had been arrested Peter followed at a distance. In the courtyard a servant girl and two men accused Peter of being with Jesus. Peter denied it three times. A rooster crowed and the Lord turned and looked at Peter. Peter remembered the Lord told him he would deny Him three times before the rooster crowed. What did Peter do at that time?

47. When Jesus was before the Sanhedrin they said to Him, "Are you the

Son of God?" How did Jesus respond?

48. Who also were hung on a cross, one on the right of Jesus and the other on His left?

49. One of the men hanged next to Jesus hurled abuse at Him, while the other rebuked the man and asked Jesus to remember him when Jesus came to His kingdom. What did Jesus say to him?

50. When the women came to the tomb where Jesus had been buried to prepare His body with spices, what did they find at the tomb?

Answers – Chapter 3 – Luke

1. Zacharias and Elizabeth – Luke 1: 5

2. An angel appeared to Zacharias while he was performing his priestly service. The angel told him his wife Elizabeth who was barren would bear him a son. – Luke 1: 8 – 13

3. He would be given the name John and many would rejoice at his birth. He would be great in the sight of the Lord. He would drink no wine or liquor and would be filled with the Holy Spirit while in his mother's womb. He would turn many to the Lord. He would be a forerunner in the spirit and power of Elijah. He would prepare people for the Lord. – Luke 1: 13 – 17

4. Gabriel – Luke 1: 19

5. He would be unable to speak until the day these things the angel proclaimed took place. – Luke 1: 20

6. Gabriel – Luke 1: 26

7. She had found favor with God and she would conceive and bear a son and name Him Jesus. He would be the Son of God and His kingdom would have no end. – Luke 1: 28 – 33

8. "How can this be, since I am a virgin?" – Luke 1: 34

9. "The Holy Spirit will come upon you, and the power of the Most High will overshadow you; and for that reason the holy Child shall be called the Son of God." – Luke 1: 35

10. The baby leaped in her womb and Elizabeth was filled with the Holy Spirit. – Luke 1: 39 – 41

11. Caesar Augustus – Luke 2: 1

12. Some shepherds in the fields watching over their flock – Luke 2: 8 – 14

13. They left for Bethlehem and found Mary and Joseph and the Christ

Child where He lay in the manger. – Luke 2: 15 – 18

14. Simeon – Luke 2: 25 – 32

15. Jerusalem – Luke 2: 41

16. 12 years old – Luke 2: 41 – 44

17. In the temple sitting in the midst of the teachers listening and asking them questions – Luke 2: 41 – 47

18. Water, Holy Spirit, and fire – Luke 3: 15 – 16

19. About 30 years of age – Luke 3: 23

20. Simon – Luke 6: 15

21. Poor – Luke 6: 20

22. Nothing, great – Luke 6: 35

23. Heart – Luke 6: 45

24. The centurion with the sick servant – Luke 7: 2 – 10

25. John the Baptist – Luke 7: 28

26. The Parable of Two Debtors – Luke 7: 36 – 50

27. 7 – Luke 8: 1 – 2

28. 5,000 – Luke 9: 12 – 17

29. Moses and Elijah – Luke 9: 28 – 31

30. That their names are recorded in heaven – Luke 10: 1, 9, 17 – 20

31. The Parable of The Good Samaritan – Luke 10: 25 – 37

32. Father, hallowed be Your name, Your kingdom come. Give us each day our daily bread. And forgive us our sins, For we ourselves also forgive everyone who is indebted to us. And lead us not into temptation. – Luke 11: 1 – 4

33. Seek – Luke 11: 9

34. Observe – Luke 11: 28

35. Dark – Luke 11: 35 – 36

36. Revealed – Luke 12: 2 – 3

37. "It is like a mustard seed, which a man took and threw into his own garden; and it grew and became a tree, and the birds of the air nested in it's branches." And again He said, "To what shall I compare the kingdom of God? It is like leaven, which a woman took and hid in three pecks of flour until it was all leavened." – Luke 13: 18 – 21

38. Repents – Luke 15: 10

39. His son was lost, but now was found (The Parable of the Prodigal Son) – Luke 15: 11 – 32

40. The Pharisees – Luke 16: 14 – 15

41. Forgive – Luke 17: 3

42. Humbled, humbles – Luke 18: 14

43. Words – Luke 21: 33

44. "Do this in remembrance of Me." – Luke 22: 19

45. Blood – Luke 22: 41 – 44

46. He wept bitterly. – Luke 22: 54 – 62

47. "Yes, I am." – Luke 22: 66 – 70

48. 2 criminals – Luke 23: 32 – 33

49. He told him, "Today you shall be with Me in Paradise." – Luke 23: 39 – 43

50. The stone was rolled away from the tomb and His body was not found. Two men appeared in dazzling clothing and told them Jesus had

risen. – Luke 24: 1 – 6

4

JOHN

Answers on page 32

1. *Fill in the blank.* In the beginning was the Word, and the Word was with God, and the Word was God. He was in the beginning with God. All things came into being through Him, and apart from Him _____ came into being that has come into being.

2. Who said, "I am a voice of one crying in the wilderness, 'Make straight the way of the Lord?"

3. What was the beginning of His signs Jesus did at the wedding feast in Cana of Galilee?

4. What did Jesus say to Nicodemus about what was necessary in order to see the kingdom of God?

5. *Fill in the blank.* A man can receive nothing unless it has been given him from _____.

6. Why was the Samaritan woman at the well surprised when Jesus asked her for a drink?

7. Initially many Samaritans believed in Him because of the word of the Samaritan woman, but after Jesus stayed with them for two days, what did they tell the woman why they now believed He was the Savior?

8. What lesson did Jesus teach when the scribes and Pharisees brought the adulterous woman before Him?

9. The man who had been blind from birth was healed by Jesus. The Pharisees questioned him as to how he had been cured. The Pharisees told the man, "We know God has spoken to Moses, but as for this man, we do not know where He is from." What lesson did the man, who could now see, teach the Pharisees?

10. Who did Jesus raise from the dead four days after his death?

11. Judas Iscariot, not only betrayed Jesus with a kiss at the garden of Gethsemane, in what other way did he sin?

12. *Fill in the blank.* Jesus said, "I did not come to judge the world, but to _____ the world."

13. After the Lord's Supper, Jesus told his disciples He had a new commandment to give to them. What was it?

14. *Fill in the blank.* Jesus said, "If you love Me, you will keep My _____."

15. What is the Helper Jesus told His disciples that the Father would send in His name?

16. *Fill in the blank.* In the world you have _____, but take courage; I have overcome the world.

17. After Jesus was arrested He was brought before this man, who said, "Take Him yourselves, and judge Him according to your law." Who was this man?

18. Finding no guilt in Him, Pilate told the Jews it was their custom he release someone for them at the Passover. Pilate asked if they wished for him to release Jesus. Instead, who did the Jews choose for Pilate to release?

19. Pilate again told the Jews he found no fault in Jesus. He became afraid when the Jews told him Jesus proclaimed to be who?

20. Pilate wrote the inscription, 'Jesus the Nazarene, the King of the Jews' and put it on the cross. What three languages was this inscription written in?

21. As Jesus was on the cross His mother was there with others, including the disciple whom He loved. Concerning His mother, what did Jesus say to this disciple and how did the disciple respond?

22. What were Jesus' last words?

23. After Jesus rose from the dead, He came to the place where His disciples were. How were the disciples filled with the Holy Spirit?

24. What did Jesus say to Thomas after he saw Jesus' hands where He had been nailed to the cross and His side where He had been pierced by a sword?

25. Why did John write of these signs Jesus performed?

Answers – Chapter 4 – John

1. Nothing – John 1: 1 – 3

2. John the Baptist – John 1: 19 – 23

3. He turned the water into wine. – John 2: 1 – 11

4. "Unless one is born again he cannot see the kingdom of God." – John 3: 1 – 3

5. Heaven – John 3: 27

6. He was a Jew and she was a Samaritan. Jews had no dealings with the Samaritans. – John 4: 7 – 9

7. "We have heard for ourselves," they said, "and know that this One is indeed the Savior of the world." – John 4: 39 – 42

8. The lesson was not to judge as we are all sinners. Jesus said, "He who is without sin among you, let him be the first to throw a stone at her." – John 8: 1 – 11

9. The lesson was not to judge as we are all sinners. Jesus healed him and we know God does not hear sinners. Never before has it been heard of that a person born blind was healed. If He were not from God, He could do nothing. - John 9: 24 – 34

10. Lazarus, brother to Martha and Mary – John 11: 43 – 44

11. He was a thief. He had the money box and pilfered from it. – John 12: 1 – 6

12. Save – John 12: 47

13. "Love one another, even as I have loved you, that you also love one another. By this all men will know that you are My disciples, if you have love for one another." – John 13: 34 – 35

14. Commandments – John 14: 15

15. The Holy Spirit – John 14: 26

16. Tribulation – John 16: 33

17. Pilate – John 18: 28 – 32

18. Barabbas, a robber – John 18: 33 – 40

19. The Son of God – John 19: 1 – 7

20. Hebrew, Latin, and Greek – John 19: 19 – 20

21. Jesus said to the disciple, "Behold, your mother!" From that hour the disciple took her into his own household. – John 19: 25 – 27

22. "It is finished." – John 19: 28 – 30

23. Jesus breathed on them and said, "Receive the Holy Spirit." – John 20: 19 – 23

24. "Because you have seen Me, have you believed? Blessed are they who did not see, and yet believed." – John 20: 27 – 29

25. So that you may believe that Jesus is the Christ, the Son of God; and that believing you may have life in His name. – John 20: 30 – 31

Acts / Church History

5

ACTS

Answers on page 39

1. After Jesus arose from the dead, for what period of time did He appear to His disciples?

2. How was it chosen who would replace Judas?

3. *Fill in the blank.* When the disciples were filled with the Holy Spirit they began to speak with _____.

4. Devout men from every nation came together in Jerusalem and were hearing the apostles speak to them of the mighty deeds of God. What was it that amazed these men?

5. *Fill in the blank.* Peter's sermon included these words from the prophet Joel, "And it shall be that everyone who calls on the name of the Lord will be _____.

6. When those at the gathering heard Peter's sermon they were pierced to the heart and asked Peter and the apostles what they should do. How did Peter answer?

7. How many were baptized that day?

8. Who was arrested because the priest, the captain of the temple guard,

and the Sadducees were disturbed over them proclaiming in Jesus the resurrection from the dead?

9. The next day after their arrest they stood before the rulers, elders, scribes, and all those of high-priestly descent being questioned. They commanded the men to no longer speak or teach in the name of Jesus. What was Peter and John's response?

10. The congregation were selling their goods and property and it was being distributed so there were none in need. A man and his wife, Ananias and Sapphira, also sold their property but kept some of the proceeds for themselves and lied about it. Peter said to Ananias, "You have not lied to men, but to God." What was their fate?

11. The apostles were all put in jail. During the night an angel opened the gates of the prison and they returned to the temple teaching. The Council planned to kill them, but were stopped by Gamaliel's words. What wise words did he use to convince them not to kill the apostles?

12. Stephen, full of grace and power performed great signs and wonders among the people. He was brought before the Council where he spoke to them, but his words cut them to the quick. What was Stephen's fate?

13. A great persecution arose against the church. Who was known for persecuting the followers of Christ and putting these men in prison?

14. An angel of the Lord sent Philip to a desert road where he came upon an Ethiopian eunuch, a court official of the queen of the Ethiopians. The eunuch was reading the scriptures and asked for Philip's guidance. As they passed some water, what was the eunuch's desire?

15. Saul was traveling in search of disciples of the Lord to bring them bound to Jerusalem. A light flashed from heaven. What happened to Saul?

16. How did Saul escape from the Jews who plotted to do away with him?

17. Why were the disciples afraid of Saul?

18. Peter was perplexed by the vision he had of all types of four footed animals, creatures, and birds when the Lord told him, "What God has cleansed, no longer consider unholy." What did Peter understand his vision to mean?

19. The apostles and brethren learned that besides the Jews, who else had received the word of God?

20. Herod, the king at this time, laid hands on some who belonged to the church. Who did he have put to death with a sword?

21. Herod had Peter arrested with four squads of soldiers to guard him. Prayers were fervently sent out for Peter. What was Peter's fate at the prison?

22. What two men were sent out on the first missionary journey?

23. What other name was Saul known as?

24. What did the Jews who had come from Antioch and Iconium do to Paul?

25. *Fill in the blank.* Through many _____ we must enter the kingdom of God.

26. Paul and Silas were imprisoned with their feet fastened in stocks. During the night the two men were praying and singing hymns of praise to God when what event happened opening the prison doors and their

chains?

27. How did Apollos, an Alexandrian by birth, refute the Jews?

28. What day of the week did the believers gather together to break bread?

29. *Fill in the blank.* Paul spoke to the elders of the church of Ephesus of how he had served the Lord with all humility and reminded them to help the weak and remember these words of the Lord Jesus, "It is more blessed to give than to _____."

30. *Fill in the blank.* Paul said, "I do my best to maintain always a blameless _____ both before God and before men."

Answers – Chapter 5 – Acts

1. 40 days – Acts 1: 1 – 3

2. They must choose between men who had accompanied them from the time of Jesus' baptism until His ascension. They drew lots. – Acts 1: 21 – 26

3. Tongues – Acts 2: 1 – 4

4. They were hearing them speak in their own languages. – Acts 2: 5 – 11

5. Saved – Acts 2: 16 – 21

6. Repent and be baptized in the name of Jesus for the forgiveness of your sins and you will receive the gift of the Holy Spirit. – Acts 2: 37 – 38

7. About 3,000 souls – Acts 2: 41

8. Peter and John – Acts 4: 1 – 4

9. "Whether it is right in the sight of God to give heed to you rather than to God, you be the judge; for we cannot stop talking about what we have seen and heard." – Acts 4: 1 – 21

10. They fell at Peter's feet and breathed their last. – Acts 4: 32 – 35; Acts 5: 1 – 11

11. "If this plan or action is of men, it will be overthrown; but if it is of God, you will not be able to overthrow them; or else you may be found fighting against God." – Acts 5: 1 – 39

12. He was stoned to death. – Acts 6: 8 – 12; Acts 7: 1 – 60

13. Saul – Acts 8: 1 – 3

14. To be baptized – Acts 8: 26 – 39

15. Saul heard a voice telling him it was Jesus and asking why he was persecuting Him. He was blind for three days. The Lord sent Ananias to lay hands on Saul and fill him with the Holy Spirit. He was baptized and

began to preach Jesus, proclaiming Him the Son of God. – Acts 9: 1 – 20

16. His disciples let him down through an opening in the wall in a large basket at night. – Acts 9: 24 – 25

17. They didn't believe he was a disciple. – Acts 9: 26

18. God is not one to show partiality, but in every nation the man who fears Him and does what is right is welcome to Him. – Acts 10: 1 – 35

19. The Gentiles – Acts 11: 1

20. James, the brother of John. – Acts 12: 1 – 2

21. An angel of the Lord appeared at his cell, Peter was awoken and his chains fell off him, and he went to the home where they were praying for him and told them to report these things to James and the brethren. He then went to another place. – Acts 12: 6 – 17

22. Barnabas and Saul – Acts 13: 1 – 3

23. Paul – Acts 13: 9

24. Stoned him believing him to be dead – Acts 14: 19 – 20

25. Tribulations – Acts 14: 22

26. An earthquake – Acts 16: 22 – 26

27. By demonstrating through the Scriptures that Jesus was the Christ – Acts 18: 24 – 28

28. The first day of the week – Acts 20: 7

29. Receive – Acts 20: 17 – 35

30. Conscience – Acts 24: 16

Paul's Letters

6

ROMANS

Answers on page 44

1. *Fill in the blank.* The righteous man shall live by _____.

2. *Fill in the blank.* Just as they did not see fit to acknowledge God any longer, God gave them over to a depraved mind, to do those things which are not proper, being filled with all the unrighteousness, wickedness, greed, evil; full of envy, murder, strife, deceit, malice; they are gossips, slanderers, haters of God, insolent, arrogant, boastful, inventors of evil, disobedient to parents, without understanding, untrustworthy, unloving, unmerciful; and although they know the ordinance of God, that those who practice such things are worthy of _____, they not only do the same, but also give hearty approval to those who practice them.

3. *Fill in the blank.* Everyone of you who passes judgment, for in that which you judge another, you _____ yourself; for you who judge practice the same thing.

4. *Fill in the blank.* Because of your stubbornness and unrepentant heart you are storing up _____ for yourself in the day of judgment of God, who will render to each person according to his deeds.

5. *Fill in the blank.* All have _____ and fall short of the glory of God.

6. *Fill in the blank.* _____ is the man whose sin the Lord will not take into account.

7. *Fill in the blank.* _____ brings about perseverance; and perseverance, proven character.

8. *Fill in the blank.* We do not know how to pray as we should, but the Spirit Himself intercedes for us with groanings too deep for words; and He who searches the _____ knows what the mind of the Spirit is, because He intercedes for the saints according to the will of God.

9. *Fill in the blank.* If _____ is for us, who is against us?

10. I am convinced that neither death, nor life, not angels, nor principalities, nor things present, nor things to come, nor powers, nor height, nor depth, nor any other created thing, will be able to separate us from what?

11. *Fill in the blank.* Abhor what is evil, cling to what is _____.

12. *Fill in the blanks.* Never pay back _____ for _____ to anyone.

13. In what way will you heap burning coals on the head of your enemy?

14. What is the fulfillment of the law?

15. Why do you regard your brother with contempt? One day we will all stand before the judgment seat of God to do what?

Answers – Chapter 6 – Romans

1. Faith – Romans 1: 17

2. Death – Romans 1: 28 – 32

3. Condemn – Romans 2: 1

4. Wrath – Romans 2: 5 – 6

5. Sinned – Romans 3: 23

6. Blessed – Romans 4: 8

7. Tribulation – Romans 5: 3 – 4

8. Hearts – Romans 8: 26 – 27

9. God – Romans 8: 31

10. The love of God, which is in Christ Jesus our Lord – Romans 8: 38 – 39

11. Good – Romans 12: 9

12. Evil – Romans 12: 17

13. If your enemy is hungry, feed him; and if he is thirsty, give him a drink. – Romans 12: 20

14. To love your neighbor as yourself. Love does no wrong to a neighbor. – Romans 13: 8 – 10

15. Give an account of himself to God – Romans 14: 10 – 12

7

FIRST CORINTHIANS

Answers on page 47

1. *Fill in the blank.* Let him who boasts, boast in the _____.

2. Who will one day judge the world? And who will judge angels?

3. Who will not inherit the kingdom of God?

4. *Fill in the blank.* All things are lawful for me, but not all things are _____.

5. *Fill in the blank.* Let him who thinks he stands, take heed that he does not _____.

6. *Fill in the blanks.* _____ is patient, _____ is kind and is not jealous; _____ does not brag and is not arrogant, does not act unbecomingly; it does not seek its own, is not provoked, does not take into account a wrong suffered, does not rejoice in unrighteousness, but rejoices with the truth; bears all things, believes all things, hopes all things, endures all things.

7. Of these things: faith, hope, love : which is the greatest of the three?

8. What does bad company do to good morals?

9. *Fill in the blank.* Let all that you do be done in _____.

10. What is the definition of Maranatha?

Answers – Chapter 7 – First Corinthians

1. Lord – I Corinthians 1: 31

2. The saints - I Corinthians 6: 2 – 3

3. The unrighteous: neither fornicators, idolaters, adulterers, effeminate, homosexuals, thieves, covetous, drunkards, revilers, swindlers - I Corinthians 6: 9 – 10

4. Profitable - I Corinthians 6: 12

5. Fall – I Corinthians 10: 12

6. Love – I Corinthians 13: 4 – 7

7. Love – I Corinthians 13: 13

8. Corrupts. 'Bad company corrupts good morals.' – I Corinthians 15: 33

9. Love – I Corinthians 16: 14

10. Our Lord is coming (and He will judge those who have not set Him at nought) – I Corinthians 16: 22

8

SECOND CORINTHIANS

Answers on page 49

1. *Fill in the blanks.* We must all appear before the judgment seat of Christ, so that each one may be recompensed for his deeds in the body, according to what he has done, whether _____ or _____.

2. *Fill in the blank.* We are not to be bound by _____.

3. *Fill in the blank.* God loves a cheerful _____.

4. *Fill in the blank.* For when I am weak, then I am _____.

Answers – Chapter 8 – Second Corinthians

1. Good, bad - II Corinthians 5: 10

2. Unbelievers - II Corinthians 6: 14

3. Cheerful - II Corinthians 9: 7

4. Strong - II Corinthians 12: 10

9

GALATIANS

Answers on page 51

1. Who is this referring to, "He who once persecuted us is now teaching the faith which he once tried to destroy"?

2. In Galatians chapter 5, nine examples of the fruit of the Spirit are given. How many of these can you name?

3. To fulfill the law of Christ, we must bear what?

4. *Fill in the blank.* Do not lose heart in doing _____, for in due time we will reap if we do not grow weary.

Answers – Chapter 9 – Galatians

1. Paul who was previously Saul. ~ Galatians 1: 23

2. Love, joy, peace, patience, kindness, goodness, faithfulness, gentleness, and self-control ~ Galatians 5: 22 – 23

3. One another's burdens ~ Galatians 6: 2

4. Good ~ Galatians 6: 9

10

EPHESIANS

Answers on page 53

1. By what have you been saved?

2. *Fill in the blank.* Be angry and yet do not _____; do not let the sun go down on your anger.

3. *Fill in the blank.* Do not give the _____ an opportunity.

4. *Fill in the blank.* Let no _____ word proceed from your mouth, but only such a word as is good for edification according to the need of the moment, so that it will give grace to those who hear.

5. *Fill in the blank.* Be _____ to one another, tenderhearted, forgiving each other, just as God in Christ also has forgiven you.

Answers – Chapter 10 – Ephesians

1. By grace you have been saved through faith. It is the gift of God. - Ephesians 2: 8

2. Sin - Ephesians 4: 26

3. Devil - Ephesians 4: 27

4. Unwholesome - Ephesians 4: 29

5. Kind - Ephesians 4: 32

11

PHILIPPIANS

Answers on page 55

1. Do nothing from selfishness or empty conceit, but with humility of mind. How are we to regard one another?

2. *Fill in the blanks.* Do all things without _____ or _____; so that you will prove yourselves to be blameless and innocent.

3. As a Christian, our citizenship is from where?

4. *Fill in the blank.* Be anxious for _____, but in everything by prayer and supplication with thanksgiving let your requests be made known to God.

5. What things are we told to dwell on in order to have the peace of God?

6 *Fill in the blank.* I can do all things through Him who _____ me.

Answers – Chapter 11 – Philippians

1. As more important than ourselves – Philippians 2: 3

2. Grumbling or disputing – Philippians 2: 14

3. Heaven – Philippians 3: 20

4. Nothing – Philippians 4: 6

5. Whatever is true, whatever is honorable, whatever is right, whatever is pure, whatever is lovely, whatever is of good repute, if there is any excellence and if anything is worthy of praise, dwell on these things. – Philippians 4: 8 – 9

6. Strengthens – Philippians 4: 13

12

COLOSSIANS

Answers on page 57

1. *Fill in the blank.* For by Him all things were _____, both in the heavens and on earth, visible and invisible, whether thrones or dominions or rulers or authorities – all things have been created through Him and for Him.

2. Where are we told to have our minds set?

3. Those chosen of God are to put on a heart of compassion, kindness, humility, gentleness, and patience; bearing with one another. Whoever has a complaint against another what are we to do, as the Lord did to us?

4. What is the perfect bond of unity?

5. *Fill in the blank.* Whatever you do, do your work heartily, as for the Lord rather than for _____, knowing that from the Lord you will receive the reward of the inheritance.

Answers – Chapter 12 – Colossians

1. Created – Colossians 1: 16

2. Set your mind on the things above, not on the things that are on earth. – Colossians 3: 2

3. Forgive – Colossians 3: 12 – 13

4. Love – Colossians 3: 14

5. Men – Colossians 3: 23 – 24

13

I THESSALONIANS

Answers on page 59

1. *Fill in the blank.* The day of the Lord will come like a _____ in the night.

2. *Fill in the blank.* _____ one another and build up one another.

3. *Fill in the blank.* Live in _____ with one another.

4. *Fill in the blanks.* See that no one repays another with _____ for _____, but always seek after that which is good for one another and for all people.

5. *Fill in the blank.* Rejoice always; pray without ceasing; in everything give _____; for this is God's will for you in Christ Jesus.

Answers – Chapter 13 – 1 Thessalonians

1. Thief – I Thessalonians 5: 2

2. Encourage – I Thessalonians 5: 11

3. Peace – I Thessalonians 5: 13

4. Evil, evil – I Thessalonians 5: 15

5. Thanks – I Thessalonians 5: 16 – 18

14

II THESSALONIANS

Answers on page 61

1. *Fill in the blank.* It is only just for God to repay with _____ those who afflict you, and to give relief to you who are afflicted and to us as well when the Lord Jesus will be revealed from heaven with His mighty angels in flaming fire, dealing out retribution to those who do not know God and to those who do not obey the gospel of our Lord Jesus.

Answers – Chapter 14 – II Thessalonians

1. Affliction – II Thessalonians 1: 6 – 8

15

I TIMOTHY

Answers on page 63

1. *Fill in the blank.* The goal of our instruction is love from a pure heart and a good _____ and a sincere faith.

2. *Fill in the blank.* Christ Jesus came into the world to save _____.

3. Discipline yourself for the purpose of godliness; for bodily discipline is only of little profit, but godliness is profitable for all things, since it holds what promise?

4. *Fill in the blank.* For the love of _____ is a root of all sorts of evil.

5. *Fill in the blank.* Instruct those who are _____ in this present world not to be conceited or to fix their hope on the uncertainty of riches, but on God, who richly supplies us with all things to enjoy.

6. *Fill in the blank.* Instruct (those who are rich in this present world) to do good, to be rich in good _____, to be generous and ready to share, storing up for themselves the treasure of a good foundation for the future, so that they may take hold of that which is life indeed.

Answers – Chapter 15 – I Timothy

1. Conscience – I Timothy 1: 5

2. Sinners – I Timothy 1: 15

3. For the present life and for the life to come – I Timothy 4: 7 – 8

4. Money – I Timothy 6: 10

5. Rich – I Timothy 6: 17

6. Works – I Timothy 6: 17 – 19

16

II TIMOTHY

Answers on page 65

1. *Fill in the blank.* For if we died with Him, we will also live with Him; If we endure, we will also reign with Him; If we deny Him, He also will deny us; If we are faithless, He remains _____, for He cannot deny Himself.

2. *Fill in the blank.* The firm foundation of God stands, having this seal, "The Lord knows those who are His", and "Everyone who names the name of the Lord is to _____ from wickedness."

3. We are given many examples of men we are to avoid. Name one of them.

4. *Fill in the blank.* All who desire to live godly in Christ Jesus will be _____.

5. *Fill in the blank.* All Scripture is _____ by God and profitable for teaching for reproof, for correction, for training in righteousness.

Answers – Chapter 16 – II Timothy

1. Faithful – II Timothy 2: 11 – 13

2. Abstain – II Timothy 2: 19

3. Men who are lovers of self, lovers of money, boastful, arrogant, revilers, disobedient to parents, ungrateful, unholy, unloving, irreconcilable, malicious gossips, without self-control, brutal, haters of good, treacherous, reckless, conceited, lovers of pleasure rather than lovers of God. – II Timothy 3: 1 – 5

4. Persecuted – II Timothy 3: 12

5. Inspired – II Timothy 3: 16

17

TITUS

Answers on page 67

1. What are older women to encourage the younger women to do?

2. In what way are young men to be an example?

Answers – Chapter 17 – Titus

1. To love their husbands and their children, to be sensible, pure, workers at home, kind, being subject to their own husbands so the word of God will not be dishonored – Titus 2: 3 - 5

2. Good deeds with purity in doctrine, dignified, sound in speech which is beyond reproach – Titus 2: 6 – 8

18

PHILEMON

Answers on page 69

1. Who was Philemon?

2. In Philemon, Paul writes what of Philemon's love and faith of Jesus?

3. What do we know about Paul at the time he wrote the letter to Philemon?

Answers – Chapter 18 – Philemon

1. He was a beloved brother and fellow worker. - Philemon 1: 1

2. That he hears of Philemon's love and faith of Jesus and the saints. Paul prays the fellowship of his faith will become effective. Philemon 1: 5 – 6

3. He was older and imprisoned. Philemon 1: 9

Non-Pauline Letters

19

HEBREWS

Answers on page 73

1. What service do angels provide?

2. *Fill in the blank.* The word of God is living and active and sharper than any two-edged sword, and piercing as far as the division of soul and spirit, of both joints and marrow, and able to judge the thoughts and intentions of the _____.

3. *Fill in the blank.* Jesus has been tempted in all things and can sympathize with our weaknesses, yet He is without _____.

4. *Fill in the blank.* It is _____ for God to lie.

5. Why do we no longer need to offer up sacrifices?

6. What happened to the old covenant when the new covenant came into being?

7. What was placed in the Ark of the Covenant?

8. *Fill in the blank.* And their signs and their lawless deeds I will _____ no more.

9. *Fill in the blank.* You have need of _____, so that when you have done the will of God, you may receive what was promised.

10. *Fill in the blank.* Consider Him who has endured such hostility by sinners against Himself, so that you will not grow _____ and lose heart.

11. How have some unknowingly entertained angels?

12. *Fill in the blank.* Marriage is to be held in honor among all, and the marriage bed is to be _____; for fornicators and adulterers God will judge.

13. *Fill in the blank.* Make sure that your character is free from the love of _____, being content with what you have.

14. *Fill in the blank.* Jesus Christ is the same yesterday and today and _____.

15. *Fill in the blank.* Do not neglect doing _____ and sharing, for with such sacrifices God is pleased.

Answers – Chapter 19 – Hebrews

1. Angels are ministering spirits, sent out to render service for the sake of those who will inherit salvation. - Hebrews 1: 14

2. Heart - Hebrews 4: 12

3. Sin - Hebrews 4: 15

4. Impossible - Hebrews 6: 18

5. Jesus was the sacrifice. Jesus did away with the need to offer sacrifices when He offered up Himself. - Hebrews 7: 26 – 27

6. He made the first covenant obsolete. - Hebrews 8: 13

7. A golden jar holding the manna, Aaron's rod which budded, and the tables of the covenant (the Ten Commandments) - Hebrews 9: 4

8. Remember - Hebrews 10: 17

9. Endurance - Hebrews 10: 36

10. Weary - Hebrews 12: 3

11. By showing hospitality to strangers - Hebrews 13: 2

12. Undefiled - Hebrews 13: 4

13. Money - Hebrews 13: 5

14. Forever - Hebrews 13: 8

15. Good - Hebrews 13: 16

20

JAMES

Answers on page 77

1. *Fill in the blank.* The testing of your faith produces _____.

2. One who doubts is compared to what, that is driven and tossed by the wind?

3. *Fill in the blank.* Blessed is the man who _____ under trial; for once he has been approved, he will receive the crown of life which the Lord has promised to those who love Him.

4. Every good thing given and every perfect gift comes from where?

5. *Fill in the blank.* Everyone must be quick to hear, slow to speak, and slow to _____.

6. *Fill in the blank.* Prove yourselves doers of the word and not merely _____ who delude themselves.

7. *Fill in the blank.* If anyone thinks himself to be religious, and yet does not bridle his tongue but deceives his own heart, this man's religion is _____.

8. What examples of acts are given for pure and undefiled religion in the sight of God?

9. Do not hold your faith in our glorious Lord Jesus Christ with an attitude of a personal favoritism. For if a man comes into your assembly with a gold ring and dressed in fine clothes, and there also comes in a poor man in dirty clothes, and you pay special attention to the one who is wearing fine clothes, and say, "You sit here in a good place," and you say to the poor man, "You stand over there, or sit down by my footstool," have you not made distinctions among yourselves, and become judges with evil motives? Did not God choose the poor of this world to be rich in faith and heirs of the kingdom which He promised to those who love Him? By your actions, what have you done to the poor man?

10. *Fill in the blank.* If you show partiality, you are committing _____ and are convicted by the law as transgressors.

11. *Fill in the blank.* What use is it if someone says he has faith but he has no _____?

12. *Fill in the blank.* The _____ is a restless evil. With it we bless our Lord and Father, and with it we curse man, who have been made in the likeness of God; from the same mouth come both blessing and cursing.

13. *Fill in the blank.* Resist the _____ and he will flee from you.

14. *Fill in the blank.* There is only one Lawgiver and Judge, the One who is able to save and to destroy; but who are you who _____ your neighbor?

15. *Fill in the blank.* You do not know what your life will be like _____.

16. *Fill in the blank.* To one who knows the _____ thing to do and does not do it, to him it is sin.

17. *Fill in the blank.* Do not _____ against one another, so that you yourselves may not be judged; behold, the Judge is standing right at the door.

18. *Fill in the blank.* _____ your sins to one another, and pray for one another so that you may be healed.

19. *Fill in the blank.* The effective _____ of a righteous man can accomplish much.

20.. *Fill in the blank.* He who turns a sinner from the error of his way will save his soul from death and will cover a multitude of _____.

Answers – Chapter 20 – James

1. Endurance – James 1: 3

2. The surf of the sea – James 1: 6

3. Persevere – James 1: 12

4. Above – James 1: 17

5. Anger – James 1: 19

6. Hearers – James 1: 22

7. Worthless – James 1: 26

8. Visit orphans and widows in their distress, and keep oneself unstained by the world – James 1: 27

9. You have dishonored the poor man. – James 2: 1 – 6

10. Sin – James 2: 9

11. Works – James 2: 14

12. Tongue – James 3: 8 – 10

13. Devil – James 4: 7

14. Judge – James 4: 12

15. Tomorrow – James 4: 14

16. Right – James 4: 17

17. Complain – James 5: 9

18. Confess – James 5: 16

19. Prayer – James 5: 16

20. Sins – James 5: 20

21

FIRST PETER

Answers on page 80

1. *Fill in the blank.* Fervently _____ one another from the heart.

2. *Fill in the blank.* The _____ of the Lord endures forever.

3. *Fill in the blank.* He Himself bore our sins in His body on the _____, so that we might die to sin and live to righteousness; for by His wounds you were healed.

4. *Fill in the blank.* Keep fervent in your love for one another, because love covers a multitude of _____.

5. *Fill in the blank.* If anyone suffers as a _____, he is not to be ashamed, but is to glorify God in this name.

6. *Fill in the blank.* God is opposed to the _____, but gives grace to the humble.

7. *Fill in the blank.* Be on the alert. Your adversary, the _____, prowls around like a roaring lion seeking someone to devour.

Answers – Chapter 21 – First Peter

1. Love – I Peter 1: 22

2. Word – I Peter 1: 25

3. Cross – I Peter 2: 24

4. Sins – I Peter 4: 8

5. Christian – I Peter 4: 16

6. Proud – I Peter 5: 5

7. Devil – I Peter 5: 8

22

SECOND PETER

Answers on page 82

1. *Fill in the blank.* But know this first of all, that no prophecy of Scripture is a matter of one's own _____, for no prophecy was ever made by an act of human will, but men moved by the Holy Spirit spoke from God.

2. What did God do as far as angels when they sinned?

3. *Fill in the blank.* By what a man is overcome, by this he is _____.

4. *Fill in the blank.* If after they have escaped the defilements of the world by the knowledge of the Lord and Savior Jesus Christ, they are again entangled in them and are overcome, the last state has become _____ for them than the first. For it would be better for them not to have known the way of righteousness, than having known it, to turn away from the holy commandment handed on to them.

5. How will the heavens and earth be destroyed come judgment day?

6. *Fill in the blank.* The Lord is not slow about His promise, as some count slowness, but is patient toward you, not wishing for any to perish but for all to come to _____.

Answers – Chapter 22 – Second Peter

1. Interpretation – 2 Peter 1: 20 – 21

2. Cast them into hell and committed them to pits of darkness reserved for judgment – 2 Peter 2: 4

3. Enslaved – 2 Peter 2: 19

4. Worse – 2 Peter 2: 20 – 21

5. By fire – 2 Peter 3: 7

6. Repentance – 2 Peter 3: 9

23

FIRST JOHN

Answers on page 85

1. *Fill in the blank.* God is light, and in Him there is no darkness at all. If we say that we have fellowship with Him and yet walk in the darkness, we lie and do not practice the truth; but if we walk in the Light as He Himself is in the Light, we have fellowship with one another, and the blood of Jesus His Son _____ us from all sin.

2. *Fill in the blank.* If we say that we have no _____, we are deceiving ourselves and the truth is not in us.

3. What must we do so our sins will be forgiven and to be cleansed of all unrighteousness?

4. *Fill in the blank.* By this we know that we have come to know Him, if we keep His _____.

5. *Fill in the blank.* The one who says he is in the Light and yet _____ his brother is in the darkness until now.

6. What is the promise He Himself made to us?

7. *Fill in the blanks.* The one who practices sin is of the _____; for the _____ has sinned from the beginning.

8. *Fill in the blank.* No one who is born of God practices sin, because His seed abides in Him; and he cannot sin, because he is born of God. By this the children of God and the children of the devil are obvious; anyone who does not practice righteousness is not of God, nor the one who does not love his _____. For this is the message which you have heard from the beginning, that we should love one another.

9. *Fill in the blank.* Whoever has the world's goods, and sees his brother in _____ and closes his heart against him, how does the love of God abide in him?

10. *Fill in the blank.* Let us not love with word or tongue, but in _____ and truth.

11. *Fill in the blank.* By this the love of God was manifested in us, that God has sent His only begotten Son into the world so that we might _____ through Him.

12. *Fill in the blank.* If someone says, "I love God," and hates his brother, he is a _____; for the one who does not love his brother whom he has seen, cannot love God whom he has not seen.

Answers – Chapter 23 – First John

1. Cleanses – I John 1: 6 – 7

2. Sin – I John 1: 8

3. Confess our sins – I John 1: 9

4. Commandments – I John 2: 3

5. Hates – I John 2: 9

6. Eternal life – I John 2: 25

7. Devil, devil – I John 3: 8

8. Brother – I John 3: 9 – 11

9. Need – I John 3: 17

10. Deed – I John 3: 18

11. Live – I John 4: 9

12. Liar – I John 4: 20

24

SECOND JOHN

Answers on page 87

1. *Fill in the blank.* This is love, that we walk according to His _____.

2. *Fill in the blank.* Many deceivers have gone out into the world, those who do not acknowledge Jesus Christ as coming in the flesh. This is the deceiver and the _____.

Answers – Chapter 24 – Second John

1. Commandments – 2 John 1: 6

2. Antichrist – 2 John 1: 7

25

THIRD JOHN

Answers on page 89

1. *Fill in the blank.* Do not imitate what is _____, but what is good.

Answers – Chapter 25 – Third John

1. Evil – 3 John 1: 11

26

JUDE

Answers on page 91

1. Who is Jude's brother?

2. What happened to angels who did not keep their own domain?

Answers – Chapter 26 – Jude

1. James – Jude 1:1

2. They have been kept in eternal bonds under darkness for the judgment of the great day. - Jude 1:6

Apocalypse

27

REVELATION

Answers on page 94

1. *Fill in the blank.* "I am the Alpha and the Omega," says the Lord God, "who is and who was and who is to _____, the Almighty."

2. What was the name of the island where John was imprisoned?

3. Who was found worthy to open the book and break it's seals?

4. Where was the seal marked on the bond-servants of God?

5. There was war in heaven. Who waged war with the dragon or Satan?

6. What is the number of the beast?

7. What did the angel say of those who worshiped the beast?

8. What are those called who are with the Lord of lords?

9. In the New Jerusalem, only those whose names are found where, shall ever come into it?

Answers – Chapter 27 – Revelation

1. Come – Revelation 1: 8

2. Patmos – Revelation 1: 9

3. No one in heaven or on earth or under the earth was found worthy. The Lion of Judah, the Root of David. – Revelation 5: 1 – 5

4. Their foreheads – Revelation 7: 3

5. Michael and his angels – Revelation 12: 7 – 9

6. 666 – Revelation 13: 16 – 18

7. If anyone worships the beast and his image and receives a mark on his forehead or on his hand, he also will drink of the wine of the wrath of God, which is mixed in the cup of His anger; and he will be tormented with fire and brimstone in the presence of the holy angels and in the presence of the Lamb. And the smoke of their torment goes up forever and ever; they have no rest day or night, those who worship the beast and his image and whoever receives the mark of his name. – Revelation 14: 9 – 11

8. The chosen and faithful – Revelation 17: 14

9. Those whose names are written in the Lamb's book of life – Revelation 21: 22 – 27

"Behold, I am coming quickly and My reward is with Me, to render to every man according to what he has done."
- Revelation 22: 12

www.ingramcontent.com/pod-product-compliance
Lightning Source LLC
LaVergne TN
LVHW021407080426
835508LV00020B/2480